Unwrapping Your Redemptive Package

By
Femi Alaran

Biblical quotations are taken from the Holy Bible, King James Version and New International Version, Crown copyright.

Published by Femi Alaran

British Library Cataloguing Data

A catalogue record of this book is available from the British Library

To obtain further copies or contact author:
Email: **contactus@litwic.org**

ISBN: 978-1-911004-01-1

Printed in England

ACKNOWLEDGMENT

I acknowledge the work of the Holy Spirit and give thanks to the Almighty God for this great privilege of writing.

I am blessed by the ministries and gifts of various ministers of God across the world. I want to express my gratitude to my father's and mother's in Faith; to name a few Pastor E A Adeboye, Bishop David Oyedepo, Dr. D K Olukoya, Dr. Tony Evans, Bishop T D Jakes, and many others.

I want to express my gratitude to the members of my family and friends for their continuous support.

To the editor and publisher for their invaluable feedback, thank you for an excellent job of editing, proofreading, and publishing.

Thank you all.

Femi Alaran

Dedication

To the flesh of my flesh and the bones of my bone, my darling wife. I dedicate this book to you.

CONTENTS

Introduction...1

Chapter 1 5

Divine Gift of Salvation 5

   What Does it Mean to be Born Again?....................6

   New Life..10

   Prayer Points 13

Chapter 2 15

Power and Authority 15

   Illegitimate Use of Authority and Power 18

   Be Sure Whose Side You are On 20

   Prayer Points 22

Chapter 3 23

Deliverance and Breakage of Curses...........................23

   Can a Christian have a Demon? 24

   Breakage of Curses 25

   How do Curses Appear? 27

     Relational Authority...27

     Generational Curses - What Door did Grandpa Open?.30

     Self-Imposed Curses 32

   How do we Break a Curse?....................................35

   Prayer Points 38

Chapter 4 39

Prosperity...39

    Power to get Wealth 41

    Unclaimed Baggage 43

    Prayer Points 45

Chapter 5...47

Divine Wisdom 47

    Living Shrewdly..50

    Don't Sow Good Seeds on Bad Soil 52

    Prayer Points 55

Chapter 6 57

Divine Health and Divine Healing 57

    Law of Divine Health...60

    God's Words - God's Medicine...........................63

    Prayer Points 65

Chapter 7...67

Divine Help and Partnership 67

    Spiritual Fidelity...70

    Allied Forces 71

    Prayer Points 75

Chapter 8 77

Unhindered Access to God 77

    No More Barriers..80

    Grow in Your Intimacy....................................82

    Prayer Points 84

Chapter 9 85

Glory 85

    Holiness, the Way into Glory 87

    Weight of Glory 90

    Prayer Points 92

Reference Scriptures 93

New Believers' Prayer..94

Introduction

A young man accompanied his boss on an oversea trip; it was his first time on a plane, so he did not know what to expect. During the flight, he sat in the economy class while his boss was in business class. The air hostess repeatedly asked the young man if he would like any food or drink. He politely declined every offer made to him. Finally, they arrived at their destination. They disembarked from the plane, and his boss asked him, "Did you enjoy the food on the flight?" The young man replied that he did not eat. The boss was shocked; he asked, "Why?" The young man replied, "You did not tell me I could eat."

Ignorance is not bliss. Ignorance only robs us of what is rightfully ours and freely provided. This book is born out of many years of spiritual growth and the desire to see new converts understanding their rights and privileges in God as new creations in Christ Jesus. At new birth, a Christian is given the *"Righteousness of God which is by the faith in Jesus Christ,"* - Romans 3:24 and is *"Justified freely by His grace through the redemption that is in Christ Jesus."* - Ephesians 2:8. We have been reinstated to the pole position God had purposed for man before his fall in the Garden of Eden. I wrote a story that helps illustrate this point.

If all we ever experience from our redemptive package is getting into heaven, then we have done ourselves a great deal of disservice. Salvation not only gives us a ticket into heaven but also helps us recover all that we have lost in the Garden of Eden. The scripture tells us, *"The first man Adam became a living being; the last Adam, a life-giving spirit."* - 1 Corinthians 15:45. The question is, what did we lose in the Garden of Eden that Christ restored to us? We won't go after the things we don't know belong to us in the first place. On the cross of Calvary, a divine exchange occurred; our weaknesses for God's strength, our misery for God's joy, our captivity for God's freedom, our foolishness for God's wisdom, our poverty for God's riches, and death for life. He blesses us by saving us from the penalty of sins, giving us victory in our daily living.

One Christmas morning, two brothers ran downstairs to the Christmas tree to open their presents. The older one was quicker in unwrapping his gifts. He was very excited, as he got what he wanted - a brand-new video game console with the latest game. The younger brother began to cry. His voice alerted their parents, who made their way quickly downstairs to see what had happened. They found their youngest son, crying, and his gift unwrapped. They asked him, "What is the matter?" He replied, with tears streaming down his face, "My brother has the latest game console and the best game." His mother motioned her son to calm down and asked why he did not open his present. The boy repeated himself, with tears still streaming down his face, "My brother has the latest game console and the best game." His mother asked him, "Why have you not opened your present?" He gave the same answer.

The boy's parents could not understand why he was crying. Finally, the parents decided to help their young son to open his present. He was amazed to see he also had a brand-new game console with the latest video game.

My story has depicted the life of many Christians who have not taken the time to open their redemptive package but are crying and are angry at others who have opened theirs. We are responsible for opening our redemptive package. Our redemption should be the highest motive for our godly living. All that we need to partake of, in life and godliness, can be found in our redemption package.

I pray that through the pages of this book, you will be able to see some gifts yet to be opened in your life. Christ has paid the price to purchase us back out of our slavery to sin, self, and Satan. The cost of our redemption communicates to us the enormous value God places on us. A slave could be freed with the payment of money, but no amount of money can ever set a lost sinner free. Jesus, our Redeemer, is interested in every aspect of our life, health, wealth, the condition of the heart, and our relationships. Every detail of your life is essential to Him. As Christians, we should never forget what God has done for us in Christ.

Chapter 1

Divine Gift of Salvation

Humanity lost its inheritance through Adam, but God restored it through Christ on our behalf. Our redemptive package is the free gift of salvation, which comes with added benefits. Many people have misconceptions about salvation. It ranges from keeping the Ten Commandments, to church membership, or doing more good deeds than bad and hoping that when we die, the scales will tip in favour of our good deeds, and God lets us into heaven. Salvation is not a dogma, doctrine, or an intellectual pursuit. Salvation is the resurrection from the dead and the rescue from eternal damnation (Genesis 2:17). The focus of Salvation is not on keeping the Law or personal righteousness; it is Jesus (Acts 4:12). Salvation is at the very core of Christianity; it is a conscious decision made when we accept that no matter what we have done or accomplished, we are still ultimately helpless and empty without GOD in our lives! *"Salvation is a Gift of Grace... lest anyone of us can boast of work."* - Ephesians 2:8-9.

Jesus made two emphatic statements in the Book of John, the first in John 3:3 *"Jesus replied, "Very truly I tell you, no one can see the Kingdom of God unless they are born again."* And in John 14:6, *"I am the way, the truth, and the life. No one comes to the Father except through me."* The first scripture tells us that our knowledge of salvation cannot be a guess work if we aim to get into heaven. The second scripture tells of how we can obtain salvation. The Journey of a thousand miles always begins with the first step in recovering all the devil has stolen from us through Adam; this is Salvation through Jesus.

WHAT DOES IT MEAN TO BE BORN AGAIN?

"If you declare with your mouth, "Jesus is Lord," and believe in your heart that God raised him from the dead, you will be saved. For it is with your heart that you believe and are justified, and it is with your mouth that you profess your faith and are saved." - Romans 10: 9 -10.

Salvation is not a feeling; it is a reality. The devil will try to make you feel that you are not saved when you fall into sin, but you must remember your life is hidden in Christ and God.

Salvation starts with our hearts, followed by professing with our mouth. There is no required age to accept salvation as long as a person knows right from wrong! Whatever point we are at, no matter where we may be, when God knocks on the door of our heart through the Holy Spirit, we must open and let Him come in and live within us. The god of this world deceives many by offering alternatives to the sacrificial death of Christ on the cross such as self-improvement, meditation, new laws, political correctness, etc. A radical disease requires a radical remedy; the only cure for sin is death (Romans 6:23). Christ has voluntarily taken on the sin of the world on the cross of Calvary. Without a connection to the source of true life, the only option is the flesh life. Most people feel an emptiness inside before their new birth, their inability to consider the spiritual side of life. The ultimate result is futility and hopelessness. *The bible says"...if anyone is in Christ, the new creation has come: The old has gone, the new is here!"* - 2 Corinthians 5:17.

With our redemptive (salvation) package comes some goodies, which includes but is not limited to, freedom for guilt over the past, freedom from distress and anxiety, all those things that trouble us, (Romans 8:2) and ultimately the fear of death, because of the eternal destiny that is secured.

Take the following steps; Jesus said, *"Whoever is ashamed of me and my words, the Son of Man will be ashamed of them when he comes in his glory and in the glory of the Father and of the holy angels."* - Luke 9:26.

1. Confess that you believe that Jesus is the only begotten Son of God

2. Confess that He has died for your sins and paid your penalty of death in your place

3. Confess that He resurrected on the third day from the dead by God never to die again

4. Confess that you accept Him as your Lord and Saviour

5. Thank Him for saving you.

Knowing Jesus as your personal Saviour and Lord is the most exciting relationship you can ever have on this earth, for it puts you into fellowship with GOD. It heals a broken relationship with God, and we can approach Him as our Father for every need in our lives (Hebrews 4:16). It is the beginning of a life of faith with the loving and most high God. Feelings come and go, but God's Word stands sure. The first thing that you must always remember is that God is not a liar. He does not deceive people. He will not use subversive tactics to get our compliance. If you have made Jesus your Lord and you hear a voice telling you that you are not saved, then the source is not from God, but satanic and demonic. Accept no such voices that contradict the assurance of God's Word.

NEW LIFE

"In the beginning was the Word, and the Word was with God, and the Word was God."
- John 1:1.

God's word is more than just a piece of literature to Christians; it is God's revelation of himself to Mankind. The storyline from the book of Genesis shows how God aims to repair the damage done by sin. Our new status in Christ comes with blessings, but it takes effort to live the reality of those blessings. A new life in the Kingdom of God begins with a challenge for us to discover the life of faith, which is seeing things from God's perspective. God's point of view is radically different from ours. We all like new experiences such as driving a new car, buying a new house or meeting new people, the only problem is our excitement doesn't last long before we find ourselves longing after another new thing. A few days after we surrender our lives to Jesus, there is the tendency to go back to our old ways. We must resist. Choose life because the only other option is death and destruction.

"You, dear children, are from God and have overcome them, because the one who is in you is greater than the one who is in the world."
- 1 John 4:4.

A man of God, David Yarbrough, tells a story of an Indian legend, about a mouse that was terrified of cats until a magician agreed to transform him into a cat. That resolved his fear, until he met a dog, so the magician changed him into a dog. The mouse-turned-cat-turned-dog was content until he met a tiger, so once again, the magician turned him into what he feared. But when the tiger came complaining that he had met a hunter, the magician refused to help. The magician said, "I will make you into a mouse again, for though you have the body of a tiger, you still have the heart of a mouse."

With our new status in Christ comes new obstacles to overcome, but we have the promise that He will never leave us or forsake us (Hebrews 13:5). Our new challenges provide us with new ways to experience God's presence in our lives. This new life does not suddenly come upon us; it is a gradual building process. We continue to grow as long as we allow Christ to be our head, and we study His word and talk with Him daily. As we learn to discover who we are, and why we are here, we can start to walk in the revelation that has been received and manifest the glory of God. We have been called to walk as sons of God (Romans 8:19).

Finally, a story is told of a husband and wife who were both doctors. One is a Doctor of Theology and the other a Doctor of Medicine. When their doorbell is rung and the house-help answers, the visitor would often ask for 'the doctor.' The house-help reply is, "Do you want the one who preaches or the one who practices?" We know the theory of Christian living, many of us preach it, but what we must do is to practice it! Change doesn't just happen!

PRAYER POINTS

1. *Father, thank You for the new life I have in You through Christ Jesus.*

2. *Father, help me to find grace and complete forgiveness in you. Help me to walk with You daily, in Jesus' name*

3. *Father, let the new life of Christ shine forth in me and draw me closer to You, in Jesus' name*

4. *Father, prepare me for Your plan and purpose for my life, in Jesus' name*

5. *Father, prepare me in every way for the challenges that lie ahead in the name of Jesus*

6. *Father, let the light of Your word enter into every dark area of my life, in the name of Jesus*

7. *Father, let the things that keep me living in the past be broken from my life completely, in the name of Jesus*

8. *Father, help me to begin to see things from Your perspective, in Jesus' name*

9. *Father, increase my faith to do Your will at all times, in Jesus' name*

10. *Father, grant me the confidence to walk as a child of God, in Jesus' name*

Chapter 2

Power and Authority

A key part of our redemptive package is Power and Authority. There is a difference between power and authority, and as Christians, we must understand both. We have a powerful enemy, but as powerful as he is, he must yield to our authority in Christ if we understand it and choose to walk in Him. So, let's define power and authority.

'Power' can be defined as the ability to do something; this can refer to our physical strength that comes with our size, the legal right to get something (i.e., the Power of Attorney). The power of a priest to pronounce a couple man and wife. Adam had power in Genesis; he was the one who gave names to the animals, and whatever name he called it, it was so; but the Authority came from God because who brought the animals to Adam to name them (Genesis 2:19).

'Authority,' however, has nothing to do with your ability or your capabilities; it has to do with the position you occupy in the hierarchy. A man who is five ft. tall could have a son who is seven ft. plus tall. In a power struggle, the son will have the advantage over his father, through his sheer size and physical strength. But the authority the man possesses as the father makes him able to control his son. Your authority gives you the right to control; this is where Satan fools a lot of Christians. He wants us to get into a power struggle with him based on our strength and forget about the authority that has been given to us through Christ Jesus. There are two Important scriptures for all Christians to remember:

> *"Behold, I give you the authority to trample on serpents and scorpions, and over all the power of the enemy, and nothing shall by any means hurt you." - Luke 10:19*

> *"And God raised us up with Christ and seated us with him in the heavenly realms in Christ Jesus." - Ephesians 2:6*

We are seated with Christ in heavenly places far above all principalities and powers of darkness. If we want to rise above our circumstances or situations, we must take advantage of our position in Christ, which is already accomplished (Colossians 2:15).

Think of the devil as a type of schoolyard bully that likes to pick on a student who he feels is weaker than him. A bully would take the weaker student's lunch money, toys, and anything else that he wanted. Like the bully the devil steals from weak Christians their health, wealth, marriage etc.

One day, the weak student's father witnesses what was happening to his child, and he decides to investigate. He gets all of the necessary information and decides to wait a little longer than usual after dropping off his son. The bully thought it was business as usual and decided to make his move on the weak student. When he approached the weak student, the father stood behind his son as the bully approached. The weak boy reaches in his pocket to give his money, as usual to the bully, but his time the bully was too scared to come close to the boy. The boy's father gave the bully a warning and made him restore everything that he took from the child. He lets the bully know that in the future, he will be watching, and if his son ever reports to him that he is being bullied again, he would be in a world of trouble.

After this, the boy plays on the playground without worrying about the bully. Whenever the weaker boy comes into the presence of the bully, the bully runs away because he does not want to be anywhere near this boy, in case the boy called his father. What changed? The weaker boy was still weaker, and the bully was still stronger. The only thing that changed was the authority that was given to the weaker boy by the one who had the power – the father– to give it. The father told his son to let him know if the bully ever picked on him again, and he would take care of him. Although the bully had no respect or fear for the weaker boy, he did fear the position of the father. So the authority of the father was bestowed upon the weaker boy, and now the weaker boy, although not having physical power, had the authority to keep the bully from messing with him. That schoolyard bully is Satan, and the father is Jesus Christ, who has given us the authority to keep the bully at a distance. We do not have to suffer through being bullied when we recognize we have authority.

ILLEGITIMATE USE OF POWER AND AUTHORITY

In the book of Acts, the nineteenth chapter, a story is recorded about the seven sons of Sceva. These brothers went around, casting our evil spirits like they saw Paul do in the name of Jesus. it reads, *"Some Jews who went around driving out evil spirits tried to invoke the name of the Lord Jesus over those who were demon-possessed. They would say, "In the name of the Jesus whom Paul preaches, I command you to come out." Seven sons of Sceva, a Jewish chief priest, were doing this. One day the evil spirit answered them, "Jesus I know, and Paul I know about, but who are you?" Then the man who had the evil spirit jumped on them and overpowered them all. He gave them such a beating that they ran out of the house naked and bleeding. When this became known to the Jews and Greeks living in Ephesus, they were all seized with fear, and the name of the Lord Jesus was held in high honour."* (Acts 19:13-17)

Demons can recognize the illegitimate use of power and authority. These seven brothers of Sceva did not know Jesus, nor did they have a relationship with Him. The devil can spot a fake Christian from afar; they pretended to be someone they were not based on something they saw Paul do. The demonic spirit said that it recognized Jesus and knew about Paul.

A similar demoniac incident was recorded in Matthew 8:28-34. In that incident, Jesus came into the country of the Gadarenes, and two demon-possessed men met Him as they were coming out of the tombs. They said, *"What business do we have with each other, Son of God? Have You come here to torment us before the time?"* In their recognition of Him and the authority He had over them. The moral of the stories is that we must not use authority when we do not have the right relationship. We will be called an Impersonation or an imposter.

Be Sure Whose Side You are On

During the American Civil war, the battles rage between the north and south, the lives of many good men were lost. A man who sympathized with both the north and south decided he would wear the top of the northern soldiers and the trouser of the southern soldiers. One day he went out onto the hill with his mixed uniform; the two armies were on both sides of the hill about to engage in battle. They were unsure if the man was an enemy or a friend, so both sides shot at him and killed him.

The story of life is a moral lesson for all Christians; we must be sure whose side we are on. The scripture tells us, *"If a house is divided against itself, that house cannot stand. And if Satan opposes himself and is divided, he cannot stand; his end has come."* (Mark 3:25-26). The book of James 4:7 says, *"Submit therefore to God. Resist the devil, and he will flee from you."* Until our submission is absolute, the devil will always usurp our authority.

Finally, I will share the experience of a pastor with you. He was a deliverance minister who was out ministering in an out-of-town church. He came in contact with a little girl who was possessed. He tried to cast out the demon in her. The demon with the girl resisted and demon in her spoke, "You cannot cast me out; two days ago, you told a lie." The pastor felt embarrassed, but the demon in the girl spoke the truth. He confessed, "Yes, he lied." He was invited somewhere he did not want to be, so he gave an excuse, which wasn't true. Somehow the devil got hold of that information and used it as a legal ground for resistance. He repented, and then commanded the demon out in the name of Jesus.

Prayer Points

1. *Father, thank you for the power and authority you have given to me over all the powers of the enemy*

2. *Father, in the name of Jesus open my eyes to see the full details of the redemptive package*

3. *Father, in the name of Jesus, I forbid the manifestation of the works of darkness in my life*

4. *In the name of Jesus, I bind the operation of the Spirit of fear, anxiety, and discouragement in my life*

5. *In the name of Jesus, I recover every lost territory to the enemy*

6. *In the name of Jesus, I take authority over my environment and city*

7. *In the name of Jesus, I bind every agent of darkness, and territorial commander over my town*

8. *I take authority over every principality and power, assigned against my life, family, children, ministry, business, career, finances, etc. I bind and render you powerless and cast in Jesus' name*

9. *In the name of Jesus, every illegitimate power over my life I dethrone you by the blood of Jesus.*

10. *In the name of Jesus, I bind every strongman hindering my progress*

Deliverance and Breakage of Curses

"And these signs will accompany those who be-lieve: In my name, they will drive out demons; they will speak in new tongues;" - Mark 16:17

The term deliverance is used to describe the process by which a person is released from the control of a demon or demons. Deliverance is achieved by driving out evil spirits using the authority of the name of the Lord Jesus Christ. Individuals can also open the door to demonic activity in their lives, through various means including, but not limited to, visiting fortune tellers, witch doctors, consulting the Ouija board, playing with occult games, studying horoscopes, watching horror and occult movies, reading demonic books, engaging in hypnosis, etc. These powers take hold of an aspect of the individual and wreak havoc (Matthew 12:43-45).

One aspect that characterises the ministry of Jesus is deliverance from evil spirits (Luke 4:18). The New Testament has many accounts of Jesus casting demons out of people. A major part of His ministry was devoted to deliverance. Jesus came to destroy the works of Satan; a prominent example is the mad man of Gadarenes (Luke 8:26-39). Believers in Jesus today have the authority and opportunity to continue His deliverance ministry to those who are oppressed and possessed.

CAN A CHRISTIAN HAVE A DEMON?

This is a commonly asked question by new Christians. The simple answer is, "Yes." Derek Prince shared a powerful illustration using the analogy of a legitimately elected mayor of a city. He is recognized as the official person in charge of the city, but you will agree with me if I said that the mayor doesn't run every aspect of the city although he is the duly elected mayor. The mafia, gangs, etc., could run parts of the city. If we think of our body like the city when we accept Jesus as our Lord and Saviour, we have elected him as Mayor but is he fully in charge of every aspect of our lives.

I once illustrated this point to some friends using categories of friendship. Every one of us has categories of friends. Some friends would knock on our door, but we do not allow them beyond the front door. There are friends who we would let in, but not let them go beyond the living room. There are also friends that we would allow into our fridge and let them eat in our home. And there are friends, like family, who can walk into our bedroom. When Jesus knocked on the door of your heart, how far did you let him? (Revelations 3:20).

BREAKAGE OF CURSES

"Christ redeemed us from the curse of the law by becoming a curse for us, for it is written: "Cursed is everyone who is hung on a pole."
- Galatian 3:13.

A curse is a negative word or an evil pronouncement against a person, or lineage, which opens the door for evil forces, or gives the enemy legal ground to wreak havoc in a person's life or bring misfortune to someone. It can be passed down from generation to generation until it is broken. Just as the blessing of God can make you prosper (Proverbs 10:22), likewise, a curse can act as an invisible barrier that keeps you from enjoying the very best of God. Almost all curses can be traced to an act of disobedience (Deuteronomy. 28:15-20).

It might surprise you to know that God was the first person to pronounce a curse on man. The bibles says in Genesis 3:17-18 *"And unto Adam, he said, Because thou hast hearkened unto the voice of thy wife, and hast eaten of the tree, of which I commanded thee, saying, Thou shalt not eat of it: <u>cursed is the ground for thy sake; in sorrow shalt thou eat of it all the days of thy life, It will produce thorns and thistles for you, and you will eat the plants of the field</u>."* A man operating under a curse is easy to recognize because he will be struggling against a tide. The person finds it hard to take progressive steps in a particular direction, what others find easy to accomplish they struggle against. There will be a consistent pattern of bad luck, such as but not limited to, humiliation, constant failure, poverty (financial insufficiency), self-destructive behaviour (drugs, alcohol, gambling, pornography, cigarettes), defeat, chronic sicknesses without a clear medical diagnosis, and miscarriages, etc.

The good news is that our redemptive package comes with the breakage of curses. Christ has been made a curse for us so that we do not have to carry the effect of curses in our lives.

HOW DO CURSES APPEAR?

"Like a fluttering sparrow or a darting swallow, an undeserved curse does not come to rest."
- Proverbs 26:2.

I want to highlight several ways in which curses come into a person's life. The scripture quoted tells us that an undeserved curse will have no landing space in the life of a person if there is no underlying reason. There must be a reason for a curse to stay. Let us look at some case studies from the scriptures that give us insight into curses

Relational Authority

The bible says, *"Jabez was more honourable than his brothers. His mother had named him Jabez, saying, "I gave birth to him in pain." Jabez cried out to the God of Israel, "Oh, that you would bless me and enlarge my territory! Let your hand be with me and keep me from harm so that I will be free from pain." And God granted his request."* - 1 Chronicles 4:9-10.

It seems like Jabez was well-off in life in comparison to the other members of his family, but he felt there was more to life than being able to eat three square meals. The enemy of best is always good. One of the greatest tragedies in life is to operate under a curse and not know. You might look at your life in comparison with those around you and feel like you are doing better, so there is no need to worry. The only standard worth comparing ourselves with is that of God. He is our marker, and therefore, He knows what potential we have.

The Bible doesn't tell us why his mother called him Jabez. In the current world, these would be some reasons why I think she might have called him Jabez.

1. Maybe she conceived Jabez as a result of rape. Every time she sees her tummy during pregnancy, it reminded her of that night, and she desperately wanted to forget both the physical and emotional pain she suffered.

2. Maybe she was a young mother or teenager whose pregnancy brought shame and disgrace; it destroyed her dream of going to university or a great career in acting. She could also have felt deserted during the pregnancy by the baby's father and her family.

3. Maybe she had a traumatic pregnancy, constant morning sickness, and she was in and out of the hospital frequently. While other women glow with their pregnancy, she was a shadow of herself.

4. Maybe during delivery, she experienced excruciating pain that the doctor offered her the option of either saving the baby or saving her life; but both managed to survive.

5. Maybe she conceived Jabez as an accident; the family already had five children, which they were struggling to feed; along comes Jabez number six. An extra mouth to feed and an unwanted pregnancy, he was not wanted.

The relational authority of Jabez's mother made the curse stick to Jabez. His name served as a prophecy of what the future would be for him. His life would be filled with pain. Wherever he went, whatever he did, no matter what direction he chose to go with his life, the result would be pain. There would always be a dark cloud hanging over his head.

"Sticks and stones may break my bones, but words can never hurt me," is the biggest lie of the devil. Words can hurt you; they can affect how you view yourself, and they can crush your dreams and aspirations. The effect of words can linger for years, but the pain of sticks and stones may last for a few weeks at the most. Parents ought to be very careful what they say to their children, husbands' need to be careful what they say to their wives, leaders need to be careful what they say to their followers, etc. The authority that relational figures in our lives possesses over us can make or break our destiny (Hebrews 13:17).

Generational Curses - What Door did Grandpa Open?

In Exodus 34:6-7, the scripture says, *"And the Lord passed by before him, and proclaimed, "The Lord, the Lord a God, merciful and gracious, longsuffering, and abundant in goodness and truth, keeping mercy for thousands, forgiving iniquity and transgression and sin, and that will by no means clear the guilty; visiting the iniquity of the father upon the children, and upon the children's children, unto the third and fourth generation."*

Are generational curses real? Parents often leave their children with an inheritance, which in itself is a good thing, but if a curse, it is then a different matter entirely. A spiritual father shared an experience with us. A young man who was at university had a severe allergic reaction to rice. He had gone to the hospital on several occasions, but there was no solution. During an event, he forgot his allergy and ate some rice; he almost died.

He was taken to a man of God for prayer, and while praying, the Spirit revealed the source of his allergy. The young man's biological father had stolen a man's bicycle. The owner of the bicycle placed a curse on whoever stole his bicycle and his children. The curse was to prevent them from ever eating rice. Now rice is an affordable and staple diet. Imagine taking rice out of your diet?

The boy was not responsible for stealing the bicycle, but he was a partaker of the punishment. The man of God asked him to make inquiries about the stolen bicycle and make restitution. Once he did, the curse was lifted with prayer.

We have case studies in the scriptures. Abraham's transgression (he lied about who Sarah his wife was to him) became Isaac's iniquity; Isaac transgressed similarly to his father before him. Jacob, who is Abraham's grandson, was also deceived by his own father to steal his brother's blessing (See Genesis 20:2, 26:6, 27:18-31). You have heard the phrase 'like father like son.' Abraham opened the door with his transgression, and both son and grandson stepped through that door of iniquity. We might try to justify it by calling it 'withholding needed information or playing smart.' When iniquity is passed from generation to generation, it becomes stronger, and unless someone breaks that cycle, it becomes harder for the next generation to break from that iniquitous behaviour.

We have another case study in David and his son, Solomon. David opened the door to sexual sin and murder, and Solomon walked through the same door in pursuit of 700 wives and over 300 concubines, accommodating all their idolatrous customs that broke the kingdom (1 Kings 11:4).

There are numerous sinful behavioural patterns can be passed on through the generations. Sexual sin is just an example; there people who have a habit of alcoholism running through the family. Some Christians have inherited the spirit of anger, fear, anxiety, lying, cheating, emotional disorders, promiscuity, and stealing spirit. The iniquities of the father are real and create real challenges for so many people in their lives. They give the enemy a legal right to wreak havoc. If you see a string or pattern running down through your family tree, then that's a good indication of generational sin or a generational curse in operation. To get out from under the 'generational curse,' you have to be grafted into a whole family (Romans 11:17-24). You are given a new name, new identity, new DNA; you are in essence a new creation (2 Corinthians. 5:17)

Self-Imposed Curses

"What if my father touches me? I would appear to be tricking him and would bring down a curse on myself rather than a blessing." His mother said to him, "My son, let the curse fall on me. Just do what I say; go and get them for me."
- Genesis 27:12-13.

A Self-imposed curse is when people speak negative words to their own life, which invites evil spirits to take over. You hear statements such as, "I am so dumb," these people find it difficult to understand the simplest of tasks. "Things never work out for me," these people find it difficult to succeed in life. "I don't think I'll ever get pregnant!" These women often remain barren. "I am sick," these people are in and out of the hospital. Needless to say, negativity has dire consequences on one's life. As new Christians, we must not be ignorant of the tactics of the enemy. The devil is a legal expert; he uses these curses to gain access into people's life legally. He then places the individual in a spiritual cage, like the scripture says, *"You have been trapped by what you said, ensnared by the words of your mouth."* (Proverbs 6:2). If you ever come across a person using self-degrading words like, "I'm so broke," be quick to correct them, "No, you're not." You might just be in time to save them from self-imprisonment.

I have had to correct people around me on several occasions on the use of words, no matter the situation we must learn to speak life, the enemy is constantly going seeking whom to devour (1 Peter 5:8). We instinctively want to use negative words based on what we see around us, but the power of life and death lies in the tongue. Jesus said, *"But I tell you that everyone will have to give account on the Day of Judgment for every empty word they have spoken. For by your words you will be acquitted, and by your words you will be condemned."* Matthew 12:36-37. The late man of God, Kenneth Hagin, shared a story of his mother, who often said she had cancer, at the slightest sign of sickness. It did not take too many invitations for cancer to take residence in her body. She died of cancer. We are told in the scripture, *"A man shall eat good by the fruit of his mouth."* (Proverbs 13:2).

When we align our speech with God's Word, we bring into our lives the blessings of God. We must remember that God takes our words seriously, even when we do not. Some opportunities have fled from you as a result of the power of your words against yourself. The evil spirit doesn't need too many invitations to take residence in your life. When we invoked upon ourselves either consciously or unconsciously, even when we are trying to assert our innocence, it could be dangerous and detrimental. Always speak life in every situation. Speak life and call the things that are not as if they are. (Romans 4:17)

HOW DO WE BREAK A CURSE?

"Having cancelled the charge of our legal indebtedness, which stood against us and condemned us; he has taken it away, nailing it to the cross." - Colossians 2:14.

You cannot be free from a curse you don't know exists or be delivered from a demon you don't know has taken residence in your life. The first step in any curse to be broken is identifying what the cause or source is? Many Christians have been frustrated in the prayer room because they have spent countless hours praying with a hit or miss approach. You cannot approach curses shooting at random and hoping to hit the target. We must consciously apply biblical principles to gain complete freedom.

I offer the following steps as a guide;

Firstly, arm yourself with knowledge. It is important to remember that all curses are broken based on Galatians 3:13-14.

Secondly, repent from all known and unknown sins. Renounce all contacts with demonic objects or religion. Destroy any demonic object in your possession. I once heard of a woman who brought a souvenir back from her holiday, unknowingly giving access to demons. Ask for forgiveness of your sins and the sins of your parents or ancestral sins (1 John 1: 8-9).

Thirdly, cast out every demon that ensures the curses work. We have three main weapons fighting against the enemy; the word of God, the blood of Jesus, and the name of Jesus. Scripture says,

> *"Whatever you bind on earth will be bound in heaven, and whatever you loose on earth will be loosed in heaven." - Matthew 16:19.*

Don't forget to bind the strong man (Mark 3:27). I couldn't tell you how long it will take to cast out a demon to defeat the curse, but you must be willing to fight to the end. I can assure you; you will have the victory at the end.

Lastly, don't leave your home empty. Scripture says, *"When an impure spirit comes out of a person, it goes through arid places seeking rest and does not find it. Then it says, 'I will return to the house I left.' When it arrives, it finds the house unoccupied, swept clean and put in order. Then it goes and takes with it seven other spirits more wicked than itself, and they go in and live there. And the final condition of that person is worse than the first. That is how it will be with this wicked generation."* - Matthew 12:43-45. Demons often operated as a gang. Take a conscious effort to stop sabotaging yourself. Two powers are waiting to act on your words; angels to work for you, and demons who want to work against you. You have the power in your mouth.

PRAYER POINTS

1. *Father, thank You for setting me free from every bondage and breaking every curse in my life, and my family*

2. *Father, every foundational curse and evil covenant in my life be broken by the power in the blood of Jesus in Jesus name*

3. *Jesus, You died for our freedom, let me enjoy complete liberty in every area of my life in Your name.*

4. *Father, in the name of Jesus, I destroy the evil pattern in my family line*

5. *Father, in the name of Jesus, my Parent's mistakes will not become my tragedy*

6. *In the name of Jesus, I command the blessings of God for my life held back through bondage to be released now, in the name of Jesus*

7. *Father, in the name of Jesus, I paralyze every evil strong man or familiar spirit, supervising evil covenants in my family line*

8. *Father, backdate the blessings due to my ancestors ten generations before me, which have been denied due to curses and evil covenant, and give them to me, in the name of Jesus*

9. *In the name of Jesus, I command every devourer and wasters of fortune to depart from my life*

10. *Father, let there be complete restoration of all what the enemy has stolen from me through bondages and curses, in the name of Jesus*

Chapter 4

Prosperity

"For you know the grace of our Lord Jesus Christ that though he was rich, yet for your sake he became poor, so that you through his poverty might become rich." - 2 Corinthians 8:9.

I think the first thing that would come to our mind when we talk about prosperity is lots of money. But we're not talking primarily about money; money is a small part of being prosperous. What use is money if you spend most days on a sickbed, or what is the use of money if your children are on drugs, or what is the profits of a man that gains the whole and then loses his soul? A man or woman who is prosperous, have good health, good relationships with others, and with God (3 John 1:2). Many Christians accumulate wealth at the cost of their family, personal integrity, and their relationship with God. If we understand that the blessings of God make us rich and adds no sorrow, then we would not make needless sacrifices (Proverbs 10:22).

Being blessed doesn't exempt us from work. God is the author of work. He planted a garden and in it He placed man for it to be cultivated. As Christians, we are expected to be creative and innovative. A prosperous man increases whatever he set his hands to do; you might have heard the phrase, "You can't keep a blessed man down." Jacob was a man that suffered greatly in the hands of his uncle, yet he prospered (Genesis 31:41). Jacob's Uncle Laban said to Jacob, *"If I have found favour in your eyes, please stay. I have learned by divination that the LORD has blessed me because of you."* - Genesis 30:27. A prosperous man has a Midas's touch, whatever he touches turns to Gold.

Man's disobedience resulted in a curse that brought lack; God intended that we prosper (Genesis 1:28). The good news is that we can be partakers of the blessings that God bestowed on Abraham (Genesis 21:15-18). The bible says, *"There is neither Jew nor Gentile, neither slave nor free, nor is there male and female, for you are all one in Christ Jesus. If you belong to Christ, then you are Abraham's seed, and heirs according to the promise."* - Galatians 3:28-29.

We can begin our prosperity inheritance through the sacrifice on the cross of Calvary.

Being prosperous also means being fruitful in every aspect of our lives. God said, "Be fruitful and Multiply..." (Genesis 1:28). Being barren is not an option in God's redemptive plan.

POWER TO GET WEALTH

Deuteronomy 8:18 tells us, *"And you shall remember the Lord your God, for it is He who gives you the power to get wealth, that He may establish His covenant which He swore to your fathers, as it is this day."*

The difference between living a life of prosperity and a life of want is choice. There are supernatural laws that must be obeyed to be prosperous. One of which is the law of seedtime and harvest (Genesis 8:22). Let me share the testimony of a spiritual father. According to him, he decided to encourage and be generous to the pastors that were under him by giving them his ties as a mantle like Elijah gave to Elisha his mantle (2 Kings 2:11-14). After he began this practice, he soon noticed that almost everyone who came to visit him from any part of the world would give him a tie or more. He became alarmed by the number of ties he had acquired. He decided to ask God in prayer about it; the Lord replied, "You are reaping a harvest of the seed you have sown. If you have planted ties as seeds, then you are reaping more ties." He came to the conclusion; the type of harvest he wants is determined by the seed he sows. He used his car as a seed, and he knew exactly what was coming back!

Some people might hear this and think this is just fables, so they don't plant any seeds. I have met many righteous Christians who are on their way to heaven but are very poor. Some believe that having money is evil; others are simply struggling along to get to heaven. Faith is the ability to see our future based on the promises and guidance of the word of God. You have to choose to believe the word of God, even if it is opposite to our feelings and human understanding. The eyes of God can see not only our past and present but also our future. Luke 6:38 says, *"Give, and it will be given to you: good measure, pressed down, shaken together, and running over will be put into your bosom. For with the same measure that you use, it will be measured back to you."* Your financial success tomorrow will be determined by your obedience to God's Word today (Joshua 1:8).

Unclaimed Baggage

"...so that we may understand what God has freely given us." - 1 Corinthians 2:12.

Everyone likes a bargain; most bargain hunters know where to go for the best deals. You will be amazed at the treasures you can find in unclaimed baggage from travellers across the world. I read the story of an entrepreneur who founded a lucrative business by sourcing goods from unclaimed baggage; his turnover is millions a year.

Christians have unclaimed treasures in heaven; Jesse Duplantis shared a testimony. According to the man of God, he was invited to heaven. As he walked with Jesus on the street of Gold, they came across a group of warehouses, one of which had his name on it. The Lord asked him if he wanted to see what was inside the warehouse. He replied, "Yes." The door of the warehouse was opened, and he saw treasures filling the warehouse from top to bottom. He was excited; in his excitement, his eye caught a little space in the corner of the warehouse, which was empty. He asked the Lord, "Why is this place empty?" The Lord replied, "That is how much you have asked for out of the provision I have made for you." He became very sad. Friends, the scriptures say, *"...What no eye has seen, what no ear has heard, and what no human mind has conceived, the things God has prepared for those who love him."*- 1 Corinthians. 2:9.

Daniel, the prophet in the Old Testament, set his heart to prayer; the angel with the answer to his prayer arrived after twenty-one days. He told Daniel he was withheld by another angel in heaven called the prince of Persia before he was rescued by the archangel Michael (Daniel 10:12). Have you ever wondered what would have happened if Daniel had stopped praying after the 3rd day, or 7th day, or 14th day? My answer is; the Angel would have been withheld, and the answers to Daniel's prayers hijacked from him. The devil is a thief who goes around seeking whom he may devour. Hence, we must be consistent in the place of prayer to claim all that belongs to us.

Whenever you forget to pray or to keeping praying, it is like leaving the airport without claiming your baggage. Don't let the devil get your treasures for a bargain.

PRAYER POINTS

1.   *Father, thank You for the prosperity plan for my life through redemption*

2.   *Father, let the fullness of Your prosperity plan be released to me, in Jesus' name*

3.   *Father, open the windows and doors of heaven over my life, let there be showers of blessings, in the name of Jesus*

4.   *Father, release uncommon wisdom for supernatural wealth upon me, in the name of Jesus*

5.   *Father, please build an edge of protection around all You have given me, in the name of Jesus.*

6.   *Father, In the name of Jesus I rebuke every devourer that wants to steal my wealth from me*

7.   *Father, in the name of Jesus, whatsoever I lay my hands to do, let it prosper*

8.   *Father, let every limitation and barrier be removed over my finances, in the name of Jesus*

9.   *Father, let there be a release of every confiscated asset belonging to me and my family, in the name of Jesus*

10. *Father, let me operate under a heaven, in Jesus name*

Chapter 5

Divine Wisdom

"And Adam gave names to all cattle, and to the fowl of the air, and to every beast of the field..."
- Genesis 2:20.

One of the things that struck me about the creation story is Adam's ability to give names to all the animals without having any form of education. He must have operated in wisdom from outside of this world. Through the ages, knowledge, and wisdom have been highly prized by civilized men. The mark of knowledgc has been the number of books they possessed and read, and wisdom the ability to solve difficult riddles and make a sound judgment. An event is recorded in the scriptures, where the authority confronted Jesus about the source of His power. The scripture records say,

"They arrived again in Jerusalem, and while Jesus was walking in the temple courts, the chief priests, the teachers of the law, and the elders came to him. "By what authority are you doing these things?" they asked. "And who gave you authority to do this?" Jesus replied, "I will ask you one question. Answer me, and I will tell you by what authority I am doing these things. John's baptism—was it from heaven, or of human origin? Tell me!" They discussed it among themselves and said, "If we say, 'From heaven,' he will ask, "Then why didn't you believe him?" But if we say, "Of human origin."- They feared the people, for everyone held that John really was a prophet. So they answered Jesus, "We don't know." Jesus said, "Neither will I tell you by what authority I am doing these things." Mark 11:27-33.

Wisdom is the uncommon ability to appraise what has happened, see what is happening, anticipate what may happen, evaluate various courses of action, then take a sensible course of action. The authority in the days of Jesus weren't Christians but was able to assess their options carefully. The sooner we realise the enormity of the task living on earth and making it to heaven, we would cry out for wisdom like Solomon did (1 Kings 3:5 -11).

The Christian life is a life of sowing and reaping. What we sow determines what we reap. If we sow in God's wisdom, we reap God's blessing and peace. If we sow in earthly wisdom, we reap death and destruction. No one can outsmart the devil in doing evil; he is a master at it. The smartest way to outsmart the devil is to do God's will. The wisdom of this world would approve of building one's life on a philosophy that is insecure and keeps changing, justifying the action based on ease and comfort. In contrast, the wisdom of heaven would be demonstrated through anticipating difficulties and planning accordingly. The Master taught us that building on a secure foundation was wise while building on the sand was foolish. *"Everyone then who hears these words of mine and does them will be like a wise man who built his house on the rock."* - Matthew 7:24.

Divine wisdom is very real and practical; what to do, how to do it, and why it must be done. Divine wisdom is more than common sense because a wise person may not always choose what the best or safest course of action is because they are not in tune with the Holy Spirit.

Living Shrewdly

"I am sending you out like sheep among wolves. Therefore be as shrewd as snakes and as innocent as doves." - Matthew 10:16

The idea of being shrewd sounds worldly and a bit unsettling for a Christian. Because the picture of a shrewd person that comes to mind is someone who cuts corners to get ahead or uses loopholes to stay in what is legally accepted without any concerns for morality. Like a businessman who knowingly exploits his partner's weaknesses or ignorance in deals. Being a Christian does not give us a license to be ignorant or be a doormat that everyone walks over. I'm quite certain that God is infuriated when we act in foolishness, or when we are on the receiving end of a bad deal. We must be wise in our dealings and do not give dogs what is sacred; do not throw your pearls to pigs. If you do, they may trample them under their feet, and turn and tear you to pieces (Matthew 7:6).

Life in this world is based on a form of exchange, and we live and breathe and move with those exchanges. No one starts at zero; everyone has something of value within them (Matthew 25:14 - 29). Take, for example, if I ask you to come over to me from wherever you are, and you complied with my request, what I have exchanged is my authority or influence through my words to get an action or reaction from you. Money is not the only medium of exchange in this world. Your integrity, your name, your personality is also a form of exchange. Solomon warns us, *"A good name is more desirable than great riches; to be esteemed is better than silver or gold."* - Proverbs 22:1. Christians must become aware of these forms of exchange so that they do not sell themselves short.

Jesus tells us the Parable of Shrewd Manager in the book of Luke 16. The main character in this parable was a man who was responsible for managing his master's affairs. He was summoned for termination by his master because he had misappropriated funds for his own purposes and pleasures. He was told, "Provide all your records. You are fired!" The manager was keen on establishing a livelihood after he was fired, and he used everything within his influence and power to make sure that it happened. He does this by giving away his master's wealth to debtors before he goes. Then the master praises him for giving away more of his money; you may ask, "What's going on?" The master's response was opposite to what one would expect. He deserves punishment, not commendation. The Lord addressed the subject by comparing the wisdom of the children of the Kingdom of God and the children of the world. He explained in Luke 16: 8, *"For the people of this world are shrewder in dealing with their own kind than are the people of the light."*

However, Jesus is not saying that deceit and theft are acceptable tools for advancing into His Kingdom. He is acknowledging that those who are in the world are more adept at using what is at their disposal than Christians. To apply spiritual shrewdness, we must use our resources such as material possessions, time, money, talent, and opportunities to build relationships for advancing the Kingdom of God. We have to prove ourselves in the small things before God will use us for bigger things. The advantage that Christians have is that we know that we have the Holy Spirit, which keeps us on the right side with God.

Don't Sow Good Seeds on Bad Soil

There is no use praying to have a better tomorrow if you're not willing to make some investments today. After all, faith without work is dead (James 2:17). If you're praying to be financially free tomorrow, what investments are you putting aside today? If you're praying for your children to succeed, what investment are you putting into them? If you're praying for a better job, what investments are you making in yourself today? If you're praying to be a better wife or a better husband, what investments are you making to develop yourself? If you're praying to grow in God, what investments are your making to grow spiritually? How many books have you read?

I was on the phone with a young lady who had lost motivation for a class she was taking in school. She ranted and raved on the phone while I listened patiently. Finally, I spoke and asked, "Do you like shoes?" She, slightly bemused, replied in a soft tone, "I do." Then I asked her, "On average, how much do you spend on a pair of shoes?" She said, "£20." I asked another question, "Would you like to buy designer shoes like Fendi, Gucci, etc.?" She replied ecstatically, "Yes." "Well," I said, "if you want to afford the designer shoes, you need a good job, that pays you a good salary, which means you went to a good school and got good grades, which means that you must pass the classes you don't like." Suddenly a light came on in her mind.

One of the keys to success is a wise investment. How should I invest my time and energy? Where should I invest my money? Important questions for all of us to ask. Any talent that is not traded will not be profitable; this is the lesson of the Parable of the Talents (Matthew 25:14-29). We are not merely Christian but also God's resource investors. We are to invest the life He gave us, and the talent and energy. As wise investors, we must understand that wealth does not occur overnight, and we must be willing to make adjustments. A man who refuses to make adjustments will find himself living stagnantly, and stagnant water stinks. However, consistent and diligent planning with follow-through will gain the necessary foothold in the future. Life is a race of individual responsibility; no one is expected to pay for your shortcomings, a lesson I picked up from the Parable of the Wise and Foolish Virgins (Matthew 25:1 -13).

Every day is an opportunity to grow in wisdom. Wisdom has influence and makes you sought after because you bring solutions to difficult situations. We are going to make mistakes, and there will be some losses along the way, not every prayer will be answered. We must be willing to take a risk at God's word; this involves sacrifice and faith.

Prayer Points

1. *Father, thank You for the Holy Spirit working supernatural wisdom in me, in Jesus' name*

2. *Father, grant me divine wisdom and creativity in every area of my life, in Jesus' name.*

3. *Father, let your wisdom take new heights of glory, in the name of Jesus*

4. *Father, grant me the wisdom to resist the bait of the enemy that will entrap my soul, in Jesus' name*

5. *Father, grant me wisdom for supernatural productivity in every area of my life, in the name of Jesus*

6. *Father, fill my heart with the spirit of excellence, in the name of Jesus*

7. *Father, let spirit of error and incapability be removed from my life, in the name of Jesus*

8. *Father, in the name of Jesus, make me wiser than my enemies*

9. *Father, grant me the spirit of discernment to distinguish between good and evil at all times, and unlock great opportunities before me, in Jesus' name*

10. *Father, grant me supernatural wisdom to help me live in peace with all men*

Chapter 6

Divine Health and Divine Healing

"But he was pierced for our transgressions, he was crushed for our iniquities; the punishment that brought us peace was on him, and by his wounds we are healed." - Isaiah 53:5

Our health determines what we do or do not do on any given day. Good health is the first wealth that anyone needs to succeed; it is the most significant aspect of our life. If you don't have good health, nothing else matters that much. No matter how big your vision is, you need good health to pursue it. The pharmaceutical companies make billions every year selling various pills to keep us going one more day. We have become dependent on artificial means to sustain ourselves. If anything happens to us now, maybe the slightest headache, the first thing we think of is, "What pain killer do I have in the medicine cabinet?" Some people, including Christians, do not believe healing is for our day. They recognise that God did some mighty healing in the scriptures, but not for us today. We live in a different time and dispensation. My question is simply this, why would God neglect such an important part of our life? Or why would He be interested in everything else, but not in our health? I will acknowledge that health care professionals are a great blessing to people, and medical science has done a marvellous job in developing the necessary cures to deal with health issues.

This book was born out of the desire to claim back what we have lost to the enemy in the Garden of Eden. God did not create man with a health flaw (Genesis 1:31). Sickness was not a part of God's plan; it was brought into humanity through the fall of man. Sin brought sickness and death, but Christ defeated the power of sin through the cross of Calvary. I wouldn't say all sicknesses are the result of God's judgment; some sicknesses are consequences of poor stewardship of our body. You cannot be a Christian and live like the world. A man who smoked multiple packs of cigarettes a day increased his chances of lung cancer. All the prayer in the world will not bring God's healing power to a person who treats his or her body like a garbage dump instead of a temple (1 Corinthians 6:19).

There are some sicknesses which result from spiritual attack. Dr. David Oyedepo once said, "Christianity is warfare, not fun-fare." For some reason, many Christians feel that their Christian life should be a happy walk in the park. We have an adversary; he desires to steal, kill, and destroy (John 10:10), and one of the ways he can accomplish this is to attack the body. We have seen examples of some of the most brilliant minds in the world trapped in an unhealthy body. One particular aspect of Jesus's ministry was dealing with demons. On many occasions, the demon behind the scene was responsible for the physical symptom in the life of the person. Until the demon is removed, the physical symptom remains. Depression in the scriptures is associated with the spirit of heaviness (Isaiah 61:3). While doctors may try to pump a person full of pills, the Spirit of heaviness remains fully in place. Until that demon is cast out, the symptom of depression will never leave the person.

The Bible makes it abundantly clear that God wants to heal His people and to prosper them in health. He said, "...*I am the* LORD *THAT HEALETH THEE*." Exodus 15:26. I would repeat the following - believing in divine healing does not rule out a doctor. Dr. A. B. Simpson said, "If you don't have the faith for the healing, get the best doctor you can afford." Walking in divine health is a daily discipline; it is crucial that we keep our eyes on the author and finisher of our faith. The enemy will strive to cloud the mind with confusion and shift our focus from Christ, our Healer. When we focus on our problem, we rarely see our solution.

Law of Divine Health

There is no one-size-fits-all solution for sickness. The solution for fixing a broken arm is different from a man with a heart attack. If we are going to live in divine health, we need to understand the spiritual disciplines associated with this. Some people believe they can live any way they want, and God's grace will override all of their actions. There are conditions attached to receiving healing and staying healthy.

The first law in walking in divine health or being healed is to know what you are up against. I am sad to share the story of a young lady who was misdiagnosed; she was treated for the wrong ailment, only to discover, too late, that she had stage four cancer, which was terminal. We must identify what the source of health issue is and plan accordingly. This makes discernment very important. Are we dealing with a physical, mental, emotional, or spiritual issue?

The second law is that we must understand that being born again does not exempt us from rules. We are responsible for the choices we make; if you break the rule, you will pay the price. It is easier for learners at school to get an A grade than to maintain an A grade throughout their school careers. God can heal, no doubt, but He will prefer we stay in health. Cleanliness is next to godliness; maintaining a good level of hygiene is crucial to staying healthy. Washing your hands after using the toilets can save you from ingesting germs or bacteria harmful to your body. A balanced diet in your food consumption is also crucial. Large alcohol consumption will damage your liver, as will high sugar, caffeine, salt, etc. This sounds like common sense, but you will be shocked to know the number of people who break this law.

The third law is work and bodily exercise. A lazy, idle mind is the devil's workshop. Your feet move in the direction of dominant thoughts, whether negative or positive. Scripture says, *"Besides, they get into the habit of being idle and going about from house to house. And not only do they become idlers, but also busybodies who talk nonsense, saying things they ought not to."* - 1 Timothy 5:13. Work to keep your mind productive and young. The scriptures command, *"...if any would not work, neither should he eat."* - 2 Thessalonians. 3:10. In addition to work, we need bodily exercise; this increases our heart rate and helps our blood flow. I found that playing a recreational sport has helped to improve my immune system drastically.

The fourth law is rest. Many don't like to rest. They have forgotten that by strength shall no man prevail. God rested after six days of creation. He commanded the children to rest on the Sabbath. He placed it as a law in the Ten Commandments. The Psalmist said in Psalms 37:7, *"Rest in the Lord, and wait patiently for him: fret not thyself because of him who prospereth in his way, because of the man who bringeth wicked devices to pass."*

The fifth Law is to learn to control your tongue. The scripture tells us that, *"Life and death lies in the tongue."* (Proverbs 18:21), not in cancer or HIV. We must control what comes out of our mouth even when we are angry or feel symptoms of sickness. *"Be slow to speak, but quick to listen."* - James 1:19. The mouth speaks out of the abundance of our hearts. We must learn to control the thoughts that run through our minds so that we are not ensnared by the words that come out of our mouth. The devil will try to infiltrate our thoughts and life with thoughts of sickness and death. Scripture tells us, *"Casting down imaginations, and every high thing that exalteth itself against the knowledge of God, and bringing into captivity every thought to the obedience of Christ."* - 2 Corinthians 10:5.

God's Words - God's Medicine

"He sent his word, and healed them, and delivered them from their destructions." - Psalms 107:20.

God has a pharmacy that doesn't close; that is His Words. God's Word is God's medicine, but it must be taken to be effective. It can be taken without the danger of an overdose or side effect. But, it will not work sitting on the shelf or under the pillow. The late man of God, Derek Prince, shares the testimony of his miraculous healing. He was diagnosed with an incurable disease, and the doctors gave him a zero chance of survival. He took their diagnosis and went in search of the scriptures. He found in Proverbs 4:20-23 the answers to his search, and he decided that he would read the scripture as he would take his medication; three times a day after each meal. There was no instant healing or any miraculous event, but within three months, what was called incurable was gone completely.

We must learn to be responsible or take the initiative for our healing. The person who is sick is supposed to start the process. So many Christians want to sit on their hands and exclaim, "If God wants me to have it, He will give it to me." Healing is a process because it reverses the destructive process or habit in our lives and accelerates recovery. Sometimes God does not take away the consequences of sin or actions but gives us the grace to endure those consequences. Apostle Paul said in 2 Corinthians 12:8-9, *"Three times I pleaded with the Lord to take it away from me. But he said to me, "My grace is sufficient for you, for my power is made perfect in weakness."* In my opinion, it is better living in perpetual health than to seek healing; we must live our lives in complete harmony with God's Word.

"Jesus the Healer is the same yesterday, today, and forever." - Hebrews 13:8. God's plan encompasses the spirit, soul, and body. His work on the cross is finished. Good health is part of our redemptive package. We must make every effort to hold onto our good confession of health and healing. We must believe the Word of God for our healing regardless of what the world thinks.

Prayer Points

1. *Father, thank You for Your health plan for my life through the blood of Jesus*

2. *Father, let every form sickness, disease, and infirmity be destroyed in my life, in the name of Jesus*

3. Father, help me to walk in Divine Health, in Jesus' name.

4. *I command every sickness, and infirmity to leave this body for it is the temple of the Holy Spirit, in Jesus' mighty name!*

5. *Father, whatever You have not planted in my body, let it be uprooted now, in the name of Jesus*

6. *Father, let there be a complete restoration of my health, in the name of Jesus*

7. *Father, in the name of Jesus, I ask You to repair or replace every damaged organ in my body.*

8. *I declare by His stripes that I am healed. God's word cannot be broken, therefore, every force holding my health be destroyed now, in the name of Jesus*

9. *By the blood of the everlasting covenant, I claim my total recovery from every form of sickness, in the name of Jesus*

10. *Father, every arrow of infirmity targeted at my body, I return back to the sender, in the name of Jesus*

Chapter 7

Divine Help and Partnership

"Now the Lord *God had formed out of the ground all the wild animals and all the birds in the sky. He brought them to the man to see what he would name them; and whatever the man called each living creature, that was its name."*
- Genesis 2: 19.

A divine partnership is initiated by God, as seen in the story of creation. God would bring the animals to Adam, and Adam would name them. They worked together toward a common vision, smoothly running the affairs of the Garden.

I was once challenged by a brother who felt angry at God. He said to me, "I don't believe there is a God, if there was a God how come there is war in many countries, where children are dying daily, how come there are earthquakes destroying homes and people's livelihood? How come there are tsunamis killing hundreds of thousands of people?" I responded using scripture from Psalms 115:16, which says, *"The highest heavens belong to the LORD, but the earth he has given to mankind."* The responsibilities of running the earth do not lie with God; it lies with man. God's plan was for man to rule the earth (Genesis 1:26- 28). But man cannot fulfil this responsibility without a divine partnership with God. At the fall of man, the devil took over the affairs of the earth and became the god of this world. He boasted while tempting Jesus in Luke 4:6 *"...All this power will I give thee, and the glory of them: for that is delivered unto me; and to whomsoever I will I give it."* You might wonder who delivered it to him. The only legitimate authority established by God before the fall of man was Adam's rule. The world believes a democratically elected government is the best kind of government. Democracy can be defined as "The government of the people by the people for the people." If there is no God in the equation, why do we blame God for the decisions made by men?

> *"What, then, shall we say in response to these things? If God is for us, who can be against us?"*
> *- Romans 8:31*

God isn't asking us to partner with Him because He needs more power or strength to make Him stronger. The Psalmist tells us in Psalms 62:11, *"One thing God has spoken, two things I have heard: "Power belongs to you, God."* He doesn't need our knowledge or research document, the Bible says, "On *the depth of the riches of the wisdom and knowledge of God! How unsearchable his judgments, and his paths beyond tracing out!"* Romans 11:33. He doesn't need our wealth or money, He said, *"The silver is mine and the gold is mine," declares the LORD Almighty."* - Haggai 2:8. He brings more to the table than we can offer. God wanting to partner with us is purely an act of divine grace and mercy. We are no match for the devil's craftiness. We need God's help more. God chooses us to be His partners to create an opportunity to bless us and transform our lives inside out and taking us to heights we will never reach by our own efforts.

Spiritual Fidelity

"For your Maker is your husband the Lord Almighty is his name the Holy One of Israel is your Redeemer; he is called the God of all the earth." - Isaiah 54:5.

Marriage is the highest form of partnership; the scripture describes the relationship between Jesus and the church as that of a bride and bridegroom (Revelation 21:2, 9). It must be honoured with spiritual fidelity. There are people with life experiences from previous relationships before they became Christians who still carry the bitterness in their hearts. They entered into the previous relationship with excitement and high expectations but ended with regrets or court cases. We cannot carry the old self into a new relationship with God and expect benefits to flow. God is not a liar; God won't make promises to His partners and fail to meet His obligations or promises (Numbers 23:19).

I was in a prayer meeting on a Saturday morning in Oklahoma. At the end of the prayer meeting, I wanted to exchange pleasantries with those around me, when I heard the voice in my Spirit of God, asking me, "Why are my people spiritually promiscuous?" The question was awkward, so I could not reply. The awkwardness stemmed from the two words -

spiritual and promiscuous. As far as I understood back then, you could not have both words in the same sentence because they are mutually exclusive. You can be spiritual and not promiscuous, or you can be promiscuous and not be spiritual. A spiritual man would be godly, not worldly. God is our Husband; like every man with a wife, He expects complete devotion from his spouse. Many Christians have one leg in and the other leg out in their marriage with God. They run after other gods, especially money, even when they claim they are married to God. You see, our fidelity to God is shown in our complete trust of Him (Hebrews 11:6). A woman who leaves her husband during challenging times is considered a gold digger. Likewise, a Christian that runs after other gods when things get tough is considered a fair-weather Christian. Our faith must be able to bear all the weather and seasons in our lives. Until our faith is tested, it cannot be trusted. Partnering with God is not a decision you will regret.

ALLIED FORCES

"Two are better than one, because they have a good return for their labour." - Ecclesiastes 4:9.

There is a high probability that we would run into trouble if we decided to try and run the race of life by ourselves. We can become self-centred, lonely, and void of purpose. There are times when we are going to stumble and fall. A partner can be there to help pick us up. No individual can function effectively by themselves; we have been created to cross-pollinate. The body of Christ is the family of God; no one should feel more important than another member. The church is healthy and grows when everyone does his or her part. Every Christian must endeavour to make the Holy Spirit a partner. A Christian asked the question, "How can I please God?" The answer is simple, learn to follow the leading of the Holy Spirit (1 Corinthians 2:11). Moses understood what it meant to carry the presence of God; he refused to move except if God's presence went with him (Exodus 33:15). His partnership with God saw one of the greatest stories of deliverance, where the children of Israel were delivered from the bondage and oppression of the ruthless Egyptians.

Wherever you see the power of God at work, the Holy Spirit is ever-present. *"If God be for us who can be against us."* - Romans 8:31. Partnering with God in spiritual warfare places us on the winning side. In spiritual warfare, there isn't anything like, 'it's a draw.' When we are on God's side, He always leads us to triumph.

One of the biggest advantages of partnering with God in warfare is that God reveals the plans of the enemy to you. His Spirit might ask you to take steps that might sound illogical. Let me share a testimony; I was working away from home for a week a few years ago when I realised my car insurance had expired. Because I was on the client's site, I kept personal activities to a minimal. I kept having a prompting by the Spirit to buy the insurance before the weekend. But in my thoughts, I said to myself, "My car is parked. I would not be driving for a few days, why do I need the insurance while I'm away from home." But, I obeyed the voice of the Lord. The weekend came; I was driving my car when the police stopped me for not having insurance. I told the officers that I did have insurance. Fortunately, for me, I could present my insurance certificate. Though their system was not yet updated, I was exonerated. If I had failed to listen to the voice of the Spirit, not only would I have been fined, I would have received points on my license, which would have affected the cost of my insurance greatly.

The Scripture records in 2 Kings 6:8-22, the king of Aram was at war with Israel. Everything the king of Aram planned to do to Israel, God revealed to Elisha in his bedroom. Elisha didn't attend any of their strategic sessions, but he knew everything that had been planned. The king of Aram was enraged, he summoned his officers and demanded of them, *"Tell me! Which of us is on the side of the king of Israel?" They replied, "None of us, my lord the king," one of his officers said, "but Elisha, the prophet who is in Israel, tells the king of Israel the very words you speak in your bedroom."* Once an evil plan is revealed, it becomes next to impossible for that plan to succeed. God is steps ahead of your enemy always.

PRAYER POINTS

1. *Father, thank You for being the ever-present help in times of need*

2. *Father, raise helpers of destiny for my life, in the name of Jesus*

3. *Father, please direct me in all of my ways by Your Holy Spirit, in Jesus' name*

4. *Father, wherever I turn, let me meet with the goodwill of men and women, in the name of Jesus*

5. *Father, deliver me from profitless labour, and confused activities, in Jesus' name.*

6. *Father, in the name of Jesus, I shall not waste my seed. Let my sowing be divinely guided to plant my seed on fertile soil, in Jesus' name.*

7. *Father, connect me to those that will move my life forward, in the name of Jesus*

8. *Father, let every Judas in my life be exposed and disgraced, in the name of Jesus*

9. *Father, you are the helper of the helpless, please help me, in Jesus' name*

10. *Father, please don't let my attitude, or actions chase away my divine helpers, in the name of Jesus.*

Chapter 8

Unhindered Access
to God

"At that moment the curtain of the temple was torn in two from top to bottom. The earth shook, the rocks split." - Matthew 27:51.

A young businessman with a great idea walked into the building of the biggest multinational company in his country. He planned to meet with the chairman to share his business idea. At the reception, he asked to see the chairman of the company, the receptionist politely asked, "Do you have an appointment?" He replied, "No, but I have a great plan which I believe he will be interested in; it will increase the revenue of the company." He was told, "Sorry, you cannot see the chairman. His diary is filled for the next three months." No matter how times he tried to explain his idea to the people at the reception, he was told, "Sorry, you can't see the chairman." The young man felt dejected. He walked out of the building with his head down, knowing full well that his plan would fail without the company's partnership. While walking out of the building feeling defeated, he heard his name being called. It was an old school friend, and they exchanged pleasantries. The friend asked, "What are you doing here?" He replied, "I came to see the chairman, but he is not available for three months." The schoolmate smiled and said, "Follow me." When they approached the guarded entrance, the security came to attention, stepped back, and opened the door. They walked into a private elevator, which led to a private penthouse suite. He knocked on the door and shouted, "Dad, are you free?" A voice replied, "Yes, son, what can I do for you?" The friend replied, "I have someone here that wants to see you." He made the introduction of his schoolmate to his dad, who was the chairman. The rest, as they say, is history. The chairman of the multinational company is like God. No one can just walk in off the street and demand to see God; He is isolated and heavily guarded. God sits in His heaven, and to meet with God, we need an introduction by someone close to Him, and that is His Son, Jesus Christ. He grants us unhindered access to the Father.

The rise of false prophets in our generation is astronomical. The reason for this is simple; there is a market for it. So many people want to gain access to God for one thing or the other. When someone claims he has a monopoly on gaining access to God, they can charge people for their service. I spoke with a lady some time ago who resided in New York. She told me that there was a prophet going around charging $500 for prophecies. The scriptures tell us that, *"In the last days that many would depart from the faith, giving heed to seducing spirits, and doctrines of devils."* 1 Timothy 4:1. If only we'd realise that unhindered access is part of redemption, we would not run to false prophets.

Two significant events took place when Jesus died; the first is when the temple veil was torn in two, which means the boundary between God and people was removed. The second is that the presence of God was no longer bound to geographic location. Friends, living helter-skelter life, trying to hear from God through an intermediary, is one of the quickest ways for us to get off balance and outside of God's Will. Christ has restored all we lost in the Garden of Eden to us; we now have unhindered access to God. The difference between those who understand the benefit of redemption and those who don't are the ones who know that the way into God's throne is through Jesus. He lovingly ushers us into the very presence of God to receive the help we all so desperately need daily to do this thing called life. Our redemption package grants us access to the Holy of Holies through the blood and sacrifice of Jesus.

No More Barriers

"Let us, therefore, come boldly to the throne of grace that we may obtain mercy and find grace to help in time of need." - Hebrews 4:16.

In the beginning, there was no barrier between God and man. I often wondered what language God spoke with man to communicate with him. There is no record of sign languages being used, God spoke to man, and he responded in kind. Sin is like a betrayal of trust, but despite the sin of man and his excuses, God still desires to have a relationship with man. He showed this in the Old Testament with the Tabernacle. However, in the Tabernacle, a veil had to be in place to save man from the presence of the Holy God. The high priest was only permitted once a year into the Holy of Holies (Hebrews 9:7). Now, we are free to come into his presence as many times as we want.

God does not like the separation, but He cannot bypass the barrier of sin. The veil in the Tabernacle is a barrier to the fullness of God and access to His throne. As believers, we can come boldly into his presence. We have an invitation and privilege to approach God through our high priest (Hebrews 4:14). Accessing God's throne with boldness means we approach with faith, not arrogance or pride, and we can face life's challenges with the confidence that Christ has gone before us. The scripture tells us, *"For we have not a high priest which cannot be touched with the feeling of our infirmities; but was in all points tempted like as we are, yet without sin. Let us, therefore, come boldly unto the throne of grace that we may obtain mercy, and find grace to help in time of need."* - Hebrews 4:15-16.

The redemption story tells us that Jesus was no stranger to the pressures, problems, and perplexities of life. He was hated and despised. His efforts to help were not appreciated. He knew hunger, thirst, exhaustion, and weakness in the flesh. His followers misunderstood Him. He knew disappointments and discouragement. He experienced loneliness and isolation. He experienced rejection and even betrayal and denial by those who were closest to Him. This tells me that it does not matter how great the challenge we face, we are not alone, and every challenge has an expiry date. Let us examine the barriers we have erected between God and us because Jesus made way for us to access God and get wisdom, strength, grace, healing, or whatever we need to move past our challenges.

Grow in Your Intimacy

"And the Lord God commanded the man, saying, of every tree of the garden thou mayest freely eat: but of the tree of the knowledge of good and evil, thou shalt not eat of it: for in the day that thou eatest thereof thou shalt surely die." - Genesis 2:16 -17.

The access that we have to God provides us with a new relationship status. Our lives are no longer governed by a list of do's and don'ts but an invitation to call God, "Our Father," with full confidence that He will hear our requests and act in their favour (Romans 8:14-16). A personal relationship with God is very different from religious practices, which are often governed by a series of motions or acts to attain enlightenment. In this new relationship with the Father, the Holy Spirit guides and leads us into a one-on-one relationship, a personal connection, and experience. Many people talk about God, some people read about God, but very few people know God and have experienced His power.

We can all grow in intimacy with God just as we do with our physical family, but it doesn't just happen. It takes effort (James 4:8). A student who receives a university scholarship to study law has not become a lawyer. The scholarship awarded only entitles him to study to become a lawyer. Jesus has granted us access, but it doesn't guarantee intimacy. I can assure you that God does not want a one-time experience with us. But our relationship with Him must be consciously nurtured and not taken for granted. Thinking back, we can all point to relationships in our lives that have died over the years from neglect. There is an adage from my hometown that says, "Twenty friends can't play for twenty years." I can think of many friends I have lost through the years due to neglect of the friendship. Good relationships are based on commitment, care, and willingness to sacrifice. If these three factors are present, then our relationship with God will reach its potential.

I had a special relationship with my biological father. Looking back now, I can say one of the reasons for it was because I spent a considerable amount of time with him - like his shadow. He told me things he probably did not say to my siblings. The more you give to God, the more you get. God will never ask us to do anything selfishly. Intimacy gives us access to God's secrets that are not freely available. It takes secrets to remain competitive or stay in business. If we want the kind of relationship we were created for, we need to surrender our wills to His will.

PRAYER POINTS

1. *Father, thank You for granting me unlimited access into your presence, via blood of the lamb*

2. *Jesus, You are the way, please lead me to the Father, in Your name*

3. *Father, cast me not away from Your presence and take not Your Holy Spirit from me*

4. *Father, let every hindrance that is stopping my new personal relationship with You be destroyed, in Jesus' name*

5. *Father, grant me unhindered access to the Holies of Holy by the blood of Jesus*

6. *Father, make me a carrier of Your presence, and set me on fire for You.*

7. *Father, let everything distracting, or hindering me from Your presence be consumed by Your fire, in Jesus name*

8. *Father, grant me the grace to be Holy in my walk with You, in Jesus' name*

9. *Father, grant me private frequency to hear Your voice at all times, in Jesus' name.*

10. *Father, open my eyes to Your glory, in Jesus' name.*

Chapter 9

Glory

"Adam and his wife were both naked, and they felt no shame." - Genesis 2:25.

The word Glory is difficult to define; it is synonymous with light, honour, accolade, success, triumph, etc. The man of God, Ray Pritchard, explains it this way, "God's glory is the total of who he is. It is God's power, love, wisdom, justice, mercy, holiness, and every other attribute of his character. God's glory is the shining forth of who God is in his essence." Hence, He doesn't share His glory (Isaiah 42:8). No human being exists consisting of all of these attributes. Scientist teaches that the Moon doesn't emit any light of its own but reflects the light of the sun when correctly positioned. With our new status in God through Christ, we can reveal the Glory of God and be a light in this dark world (Matthew

5:14). Jesus said, *"The glory which You have given Me I have given to them, that they may be one, just as We are one."*- John 17:22-24. Adam and Eve felt no shame in the Garden of Eden because of the manifest presence of God that was in abundance. When sin entered into humanity, God's presence evaporated from man, leaving man in shame and confusion. God's plan for man is to reflect His glory. It is a beautiful, but a frightening thing, to come to the glory of God. When Adam fell from glory, instead of wanting to meet with God, man became afraid of God. He hid from His presence, covering himself up with leaves.

God called us before He created this world with a purpose and destiny that He wants us to fulfil. As we begin to find out who we are and why we are here, we can start to walk in that revelation and manifest the glory of God. I believe there is an identity crisis within the body of Christ. Satan doesn't have any new tricks; he recycles the old ones in different forms. It is not a coincidence that he asked Jesus, *"If you are the Son of God, tell these stones to become bread."* - Matthew 4:3. He was not interested in the bread; he was curious if Jesus knew who he was. The irony of the temptation is that the previous chapter ended with a public announcement of who Jesus is, *"This is my Son, whom I love; with him, I am well pleased."* - Matthew 3:17. The devil is terrified of people who know who they are and carry God's manifest presence.

I appreciate that we are all at different places in our growth and maturity in Christ, but we must have a mind-set different from the world. We must not look back at the past. Too many Christians dwell incessantly on past mistakes and failures. You have been forgiven for the past, but you will be held accountable for what you are doing right now. Don't let the past rob you of the present, and ultimately, your future. Some Christians are discouraged because they have unbiblical expectations of a trouble-free life. They say things like, "If I am a child of God, how come I still get sick?" "How come I still suffer pain?" Jesus said, *"I have told you these things, so that in me you may have peace. In this world, you will have trouble. But take heart! I have overcome the world."*- John 16:33

HOLINESS, THE WAY INTO GLORY

God can't sin. Holiness is the very nature of God. His plans, thoughts, disposition, judgment, throne, and angels, everything about God is Holy. For this reason, God demands holiness from His people. It is unfortunate that many people, including Christians, view holiness as a deprivation of pleasure. Our modern definition of holiness means the absence of the pleasures of life; this could not be further from the truth (Job 36:11). The simplest definition of holiness is being of one mind with God, hating what He hates, loving what He loves, and judging everything in this world by the standard of His Word. It is the character and conduct of the new creature we are in Him. It is the power of the Holy Spirit working in our lives, helping us to submit to the will of the Almighty God. If we are going to see His glory, we have no choice after salvation but to press on to holiness as the nature of God forbids every form of ungodliness.

Holiness is much more than having good manners and godly characters. Holiness makes us possess the divine nature of God, which gives us authority over the devil (Psalms 114). It keeps us from struggling with sin, which robs us of His glory.

One of the most famous equations of Albert Einstein is $E=MC^2$. The formula can be defined as energy equals mass times the speed of light, squared. The formula is the basis for bombs or weapons of mass destruction. If we juxtaposed the formula into a spiritual context, we take M to represent man in a Pure and Holy state, C to the presence or the power of God, squared; the amount of glory a man will then exhibit will be astronomical. We cannot underestimate what God can do in our lives when we are willing to surrender all to Him.

Our status as sinners was so severe, to the point that God had to send His Son as a sacrifice to save us. The reason we are not serious about our sin is that we don't have an idea of how loving, and at the same time, righteous God is. God's presence in our lives reveals the ugliness of our sin. If you and I think we can be accepted and saved by our kind acts, you are mistaken in two things. 1) You are underestimating God's standard for righteousness. 2) You are overestimating your capability to do righteousness (Isaiah 64:6).

Then Moses said to him, *"If your Presence does not go with us, do not send us up from here."* Exodus 33:15.

Moses had seen first-hand the awesome power of God's presence and what it meant to have His presence withdrawn. When we become carriers of his presence, we become irresistible and untouchable. We have examples of people who carried God's presence in the scripture. We have Daniel in the lion's den; the lions could not harm him. We have Joseph in prison, he found favour, though accused of trying to rape his master's wife. We have Shadrach, Meshach, and Abednego in the fiery furnace, and the fire could not burn them. You see, when the devil entices us into sin, he is trying endlessly to remove the presence of God from our lives, which can leave us like sitting duck's waiting for hunters' bullet.

WEIGHT OF GLORY

Then Moses said, *"Now show me your glory."* - Exodus 33:18.

The revelation of God's glory comes at a personal cost. Sometimes we pray, and we ask for things that we cannot receive. The strength of the structure determines the weight it can support, or the whole building will collapse. We want certain blessings, but we have no idea of the cost involved. Think about it, when you order a cup of coffee from a place like Starbucks, you would be asked what size you preferred? Your options are Tall, Grande, Venti, and Trenta. The difference between the sizes is their capacity to hold or contain more. I believe that God has the ability and the willingness to bless us abundantly above all that we could ever think or ask (Ephesians 3:20). There is no shortage of resources with God. The problem lies here on earth and our capacity to receive. Here is a prayer I have learned to pray. "Lord, increase my capacity." God is not fair, but God is just. He gives every man according to his capacity (Matthew 25:15). Don't ask for more if you are not ready for the responsibility that comes with it, as with great power comes great responsibilities. You must use what you have first before you are qualified to receive more. In the Parable of the Talent, the servant who failed to use what he had been given was regarded as being wicked (Matthew 25: 14 -30).

Finally, a surplus is not a valid reason for waste. A common theme that runs through the scripture is that God hates waste. In the story of the Widow and the miracle of the Olive Oil; when there were no more jars to pour the oil into the Olive oil ceased to flow (2 kings 4:6). Another example is when God fed the Israelites with manna. He told them to collect what they could eat for the day and not waste. When Jesus fed the five thousand, He asked them to collect the fragments (Matthew 14:13-21). The Lord has promised in Haggai 2:9, *"The glory of this latter house shall be greater than of the former, saith the LORD of hosts."*

I believe that the Lord has opened your eyes and increased your faith through the pages of this book. You cannot go beyond what you cannot see, and you cannot claim what you don't know to belong to you. Our redemptive package comes with far more blessings than we can imagine, so let us think of possibilities and remove the limitations, for everything is possible for him who believes.

God bless you.

Prayer Points

1. *Father, thank You for revealing the truth of Your word and glory to me.*

2. *Father, please show me Your glory. Take me behind the veil, in Jesus' name.*

3. *Father, let Your manifest presence go with me everywhere I go, in Jesus' name.*

4. *Father Lord, make Your ways known to me, in Jesus' name.*

5. *Father, teach me to align myself with Your will and word at all times, in Jesus' name.*

6. *Father, grant me a deeper level of intimacy with You and the Holy Spirit, in Jesus' name.*

7. *Father, please increase my capacity. I want more, in Jesus' name.*

8. *Father, let every hardness in my heart, and soul be destroyed, give me a heart of flesh, in Jesus' name.*

9. *Father, give me platforms and opportunities to showcase my talents and giftings, in Jesus' name*

10. *Father, please block every leaking hole in my pocket and every waste in my life, in Jesus' name*

REFERENCE SCRIPTURES

"All that the Father giveth me shall come to me; and him that cometh to me I will in no wise cast out." - John 6:37.

"That if thou shalt confess with thy mouth the Lord Jesus, and shalt believe in thine heart that God hath raised him from the dead, thou shalt be saved. For with the heart, man believeth unto righteousness; and with the mouth, confession is made unto salvation." - Romans 10:9-10.

"Therefore, if any man is in Christ, he is a new creature: old things are passed away; behold, all things have become new." - 2 Corinthians 5:17.

New Believers' Prayer

Dear Heavenly Father,

I come to You today as a sinner. I believe You sent Your Son Jesus to die on the cross for my sins, and on the third day, he rose from the grave. You promised that whosoever comes to You; You will not reject that person. I now believe this promise, and I come to You in the name of Jesus. Please forgive me of all my sins and unrighteousness. I accept Jesus as my Lord and Personal Saviour. Please write my name in your book of life. Thank You, Father, for saving me In Jesus' name. Amen.

Name: _______________________________________

Date: _______________________________________

Signed: _____________________________________